Laws of Electrolysis! What is Electrolysis and More

Chemistry for Kids

Children's Chemistry Books

pfiffikus

EDUCATIONAL BOOKS FOR CHILDREN K-12

What is electrolysis?
What are the laws of electrolysis?
How is it done?

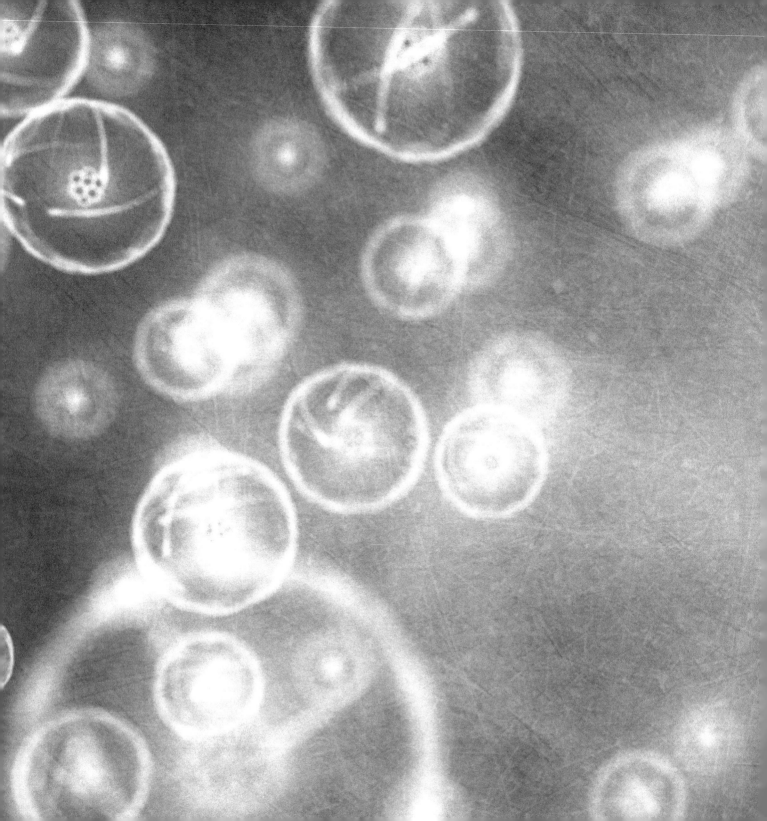

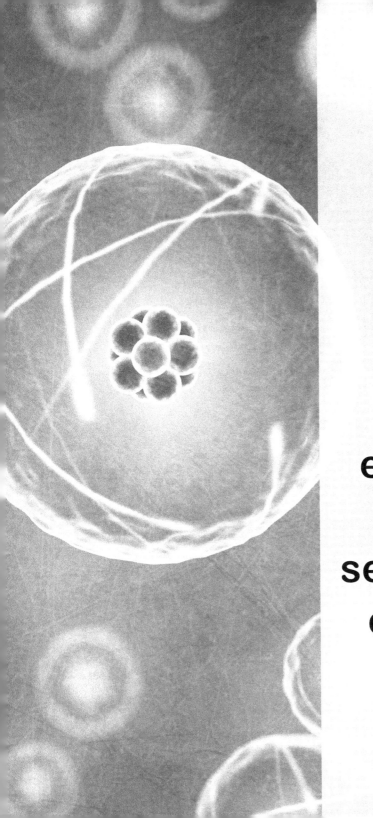

Electrolysis is a systematic way of splitting substances. It is also called electric-splitting. Substances are separated using an electric current.

Electrolysis is a process of producing a chemical change by passing an electrical current through a liquid. Yes, this process uses electric energy.

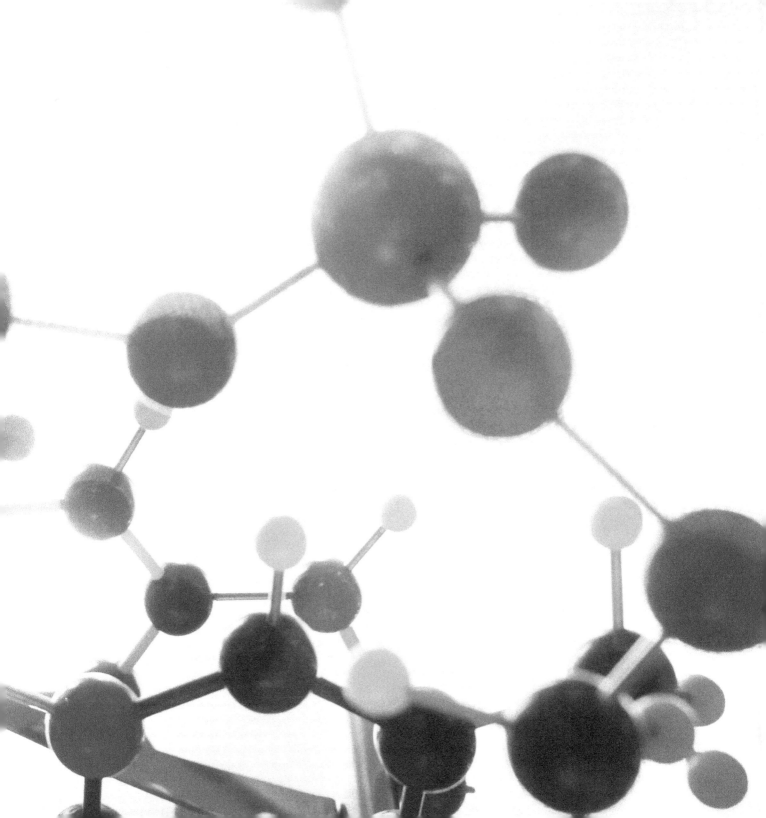

C8H

8C3HIII

... ion laboramus eu, id solet mucius quo. Verear
... eu eos dolor accusamus.

In chemistry, electrolysis is used to separate a liquid into its chemical parts. It is done by passing an electric current through the liquid.

How is electrolysis done? Let's try with water. We need a container of water, a source of direct current, or DC, two electrodes and an electrolyte to help transmit the charge.

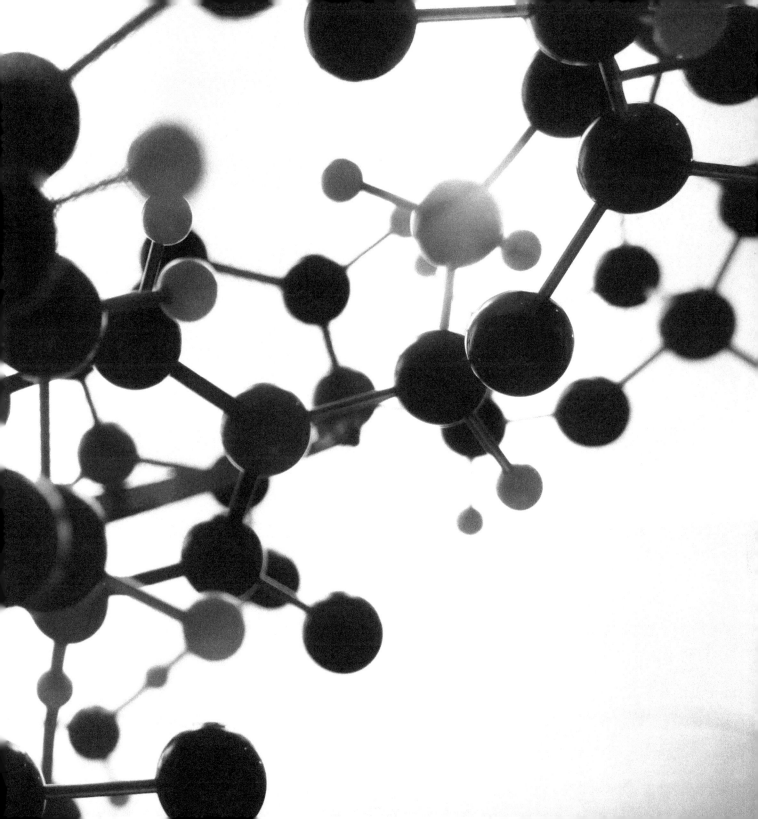

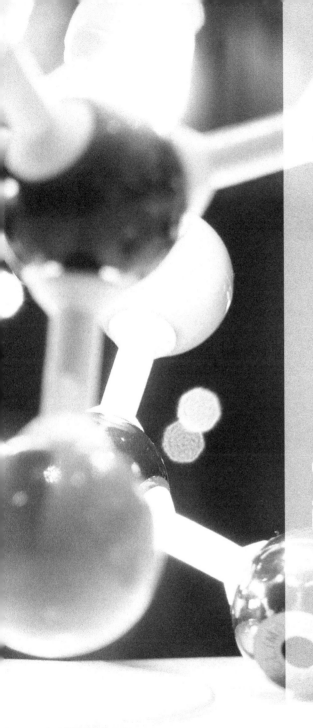

The battery, which is the source of the current, is attached to strips of platinum metal which act as the electrodes and are immersed in water, with a few drops of sulfuric acid as the electrolyte.

One electrode is attached to the positive pole of the battery, and the other to the negative pole. They are separated from each other in the solution. Electricity will go through the cathode, or the negatively charged electrode.

Then, the positively charged parts of the solution will travel to the cathode and combined with its electrons. These are converted into neutral molecules.

The process of electrolysis is used in different human activities. The mining industry uses electrolysis in separating reactive metals from the ore they are found in.

The cathode is the negatively charged electrode. The anode is the positively charged electrode. Both of them attract the ions of the opposite charge charge. In the process, the negative ions go to the anode or the positive electrode. The positively charged parts go to the cathode or negative electrode. Neutral molecules are formed.

The most popular example of electrolysis is the breakdown of water into its parts by means of an electric current. What are the components of water? Water is hydrogen and oxygen, so electrolysis splits the so hydrogen and oxygen gases are produced.

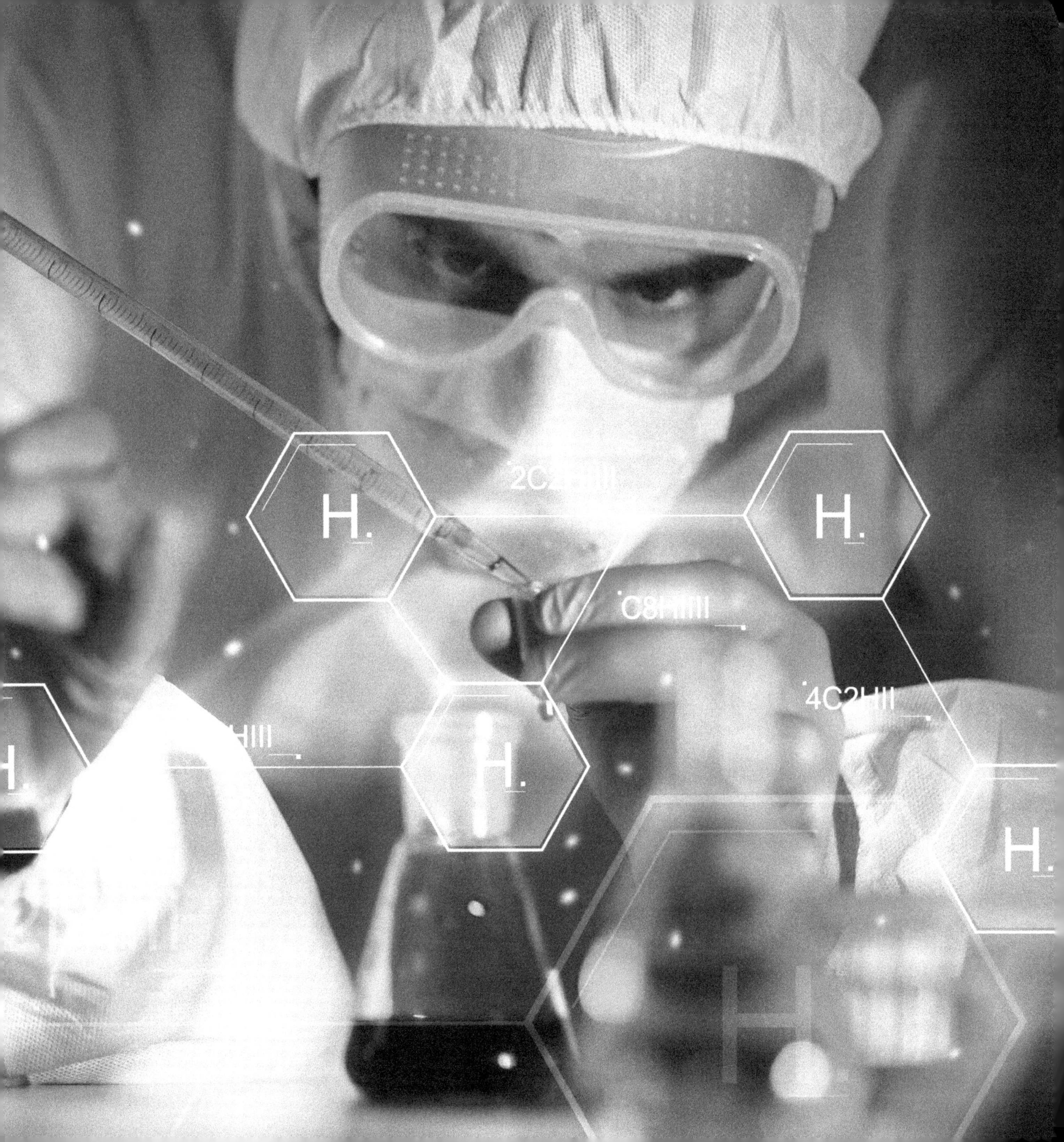
H.
H.
H.
H.
H.

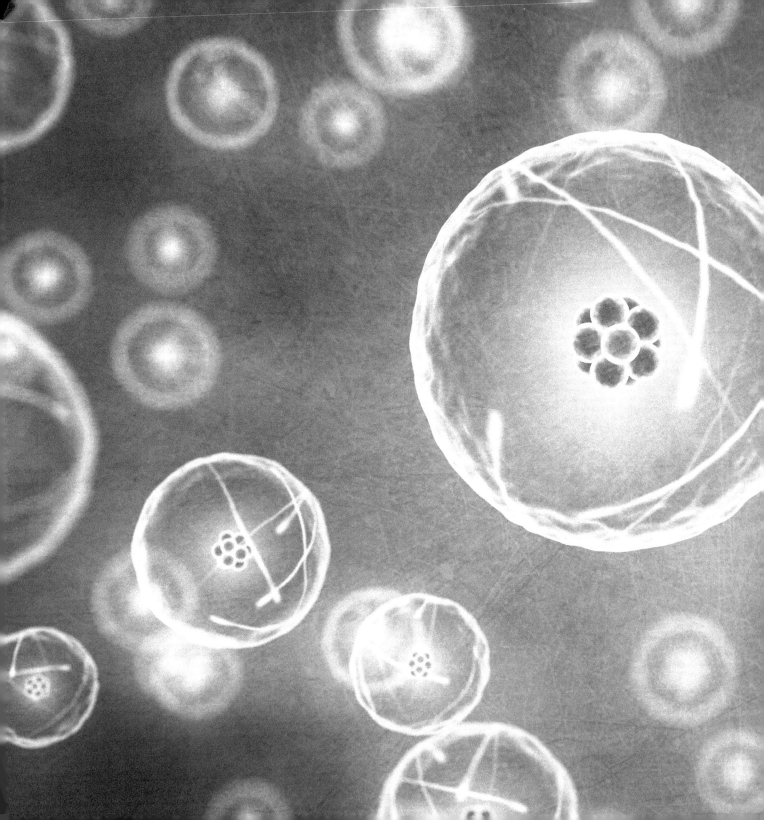

In copper chloride electrolysis, an electric current is used to split the solution to produce copper and chlorine gas.

First Law of Electrolysis

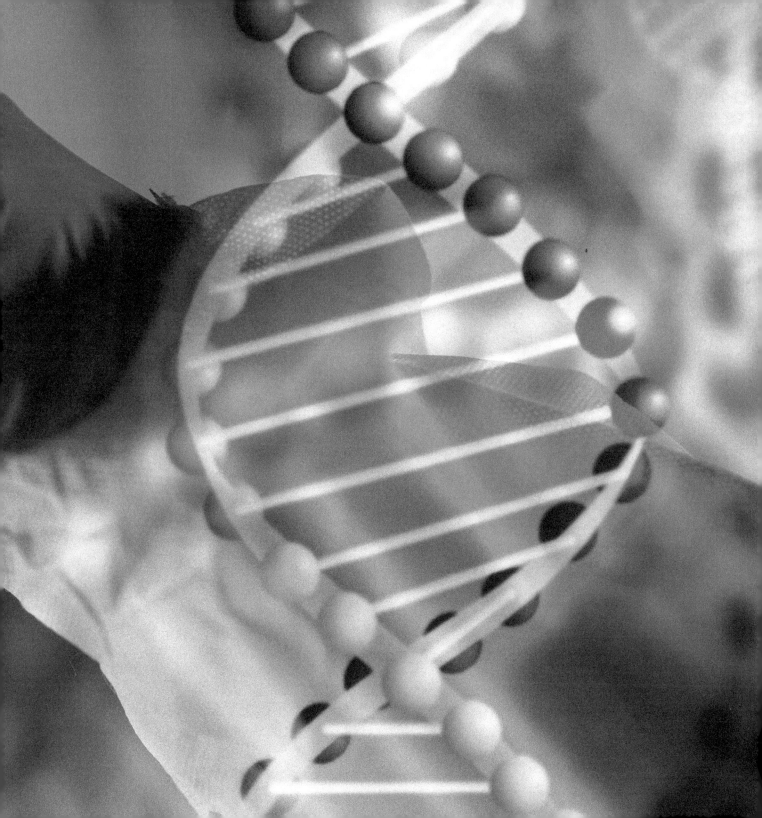

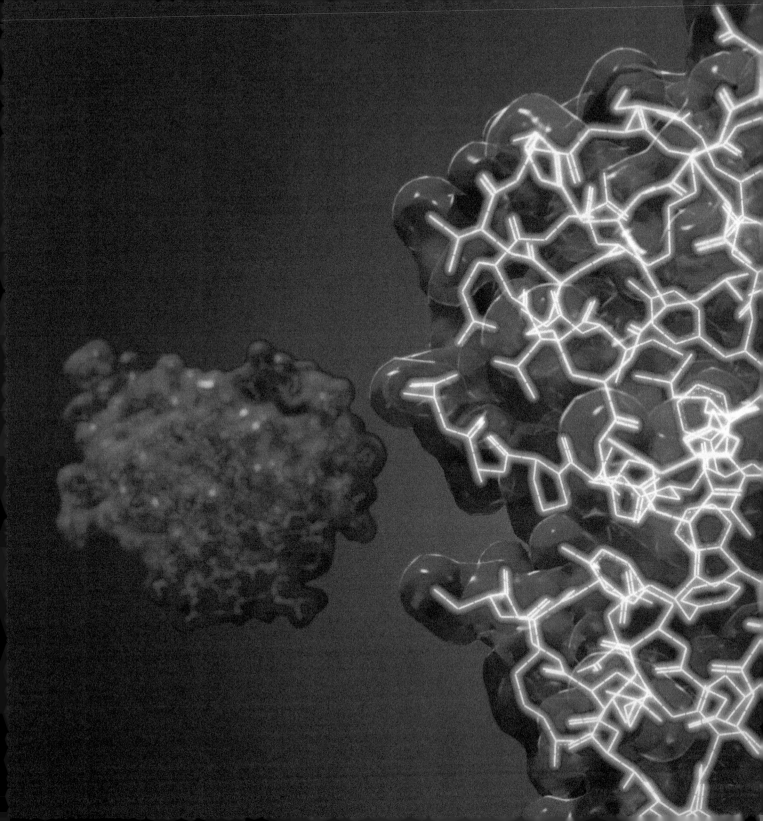

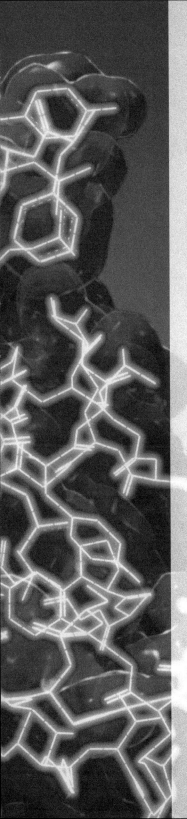

Michael Faraday, an English physicist, reported the basis of the first law of electrolysis. He concluded that the quantity of elements separated, or the chemical deposits, due to an electric current was directly proportional to the quantity of electricity or current passed through the electrolyte.

In other words, the first law of electrolysis states that the mass of chemical deposits or dissolved substance at any electrode is proportional to the quantity of electric current passed through the solution.

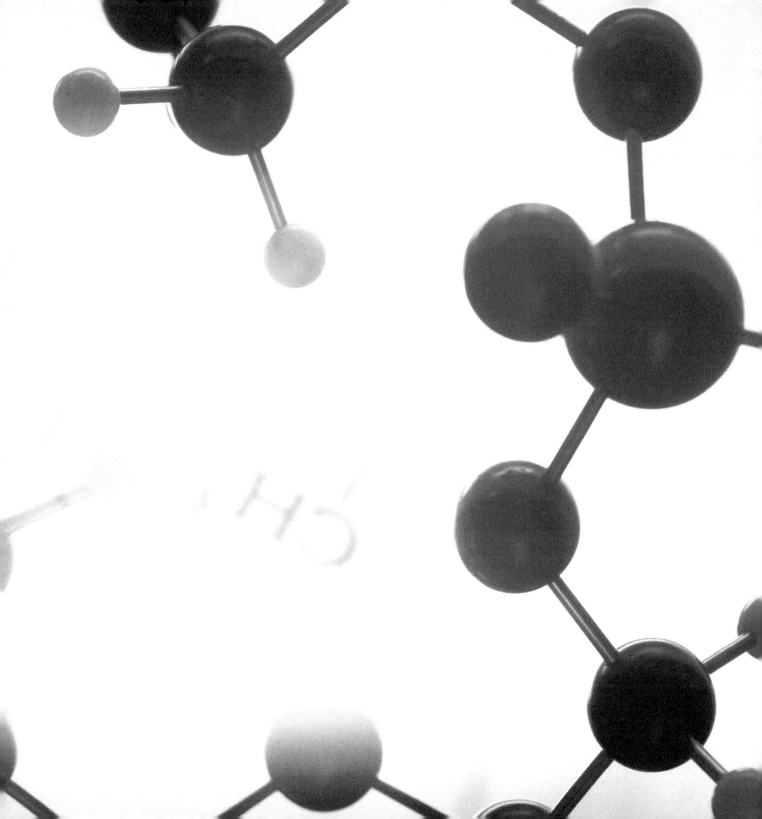

Second Law of Electrolysis

The second law follows the first law of electrolysis, but includes the substance's atomic weight. It states that the mass of the chemical or dissolved substance is not only proportional to the quantity of electricity but also to their equivalent masses or weight.

Therefore, when a number of electrolytic solutions are passed through by the same quantity of electricity, the masses of the materials dissolved at the electrodes are directly proportional to their equivalent masses.

There is more to learn about the laws of electrolysis. Research and have fun!

CPSIA information can be obtained
at www.ICGtesting.com
Printed in the USA
LVHW061159270720
661624LV00015B/960